Without Penalty

J.B. Jones

Without Penalty   J.B. Jones

Copyright © 2018 by J.B. Jones

All rights reserved. No part of this book may be reproduced in any form without written permission from the publishers, except by reviewers and authors, who may quote brief passages in a review to be printed in a book, newspaper or magazine.

ISBN-13: 978-1-944583-24-8

Published by Laurel Rose Publishing

www.laurelrosepublishing.com

laurelrosepublishing@gmail.com

Without Penalty   J.B. Jones

Contents

FORWARD	4
1 The Murder of Sheriff J.M. Poag	6
2 The Aftermath	19
3 The Mob Trials: Arraignment	38
4 The Murder of O.R. "Buster" Thomason	45
5 The 1904 Trial of James "Jim" Whitt	50
6 The 1905 Trial of James "Jim" Whitt	64
7 The Final Trial of James Whitt	77
8 The Mob Trials	82
9 Without Penalty	95
Bibliography	100
About The Author	108

Without Penalty — J.B. Jones

FORWARD

It is no secret that I have an affinity for things of old. Bringing people back to life by the telling of their story is something that I love. Every single person that has ever lived has a story to tell. Of course, some people prove to have a more interesting story to tell than others, but there is always a story. Over the summer, I suppose I was looking for inspiration. It can come in the strangest ways. Out of boredom, I typed "Senatobia" in the
Search bar on Newspapers.com. To my surprise, there were tons of newspaper articles featuring the city of Senatobia. One particular story that appeared over and over again was the murder of Sheriff John Macon Poag in April 1905. It was apparently a huge story for the time. The story of his murder was featured in over 30 newspapers all across the United States including papers in New York, California, Washington, and everywhere in between. I could not help myself to find out what happened. The newspapers were clear that a mob had attempted to gain access to the Tate County Jail in a failed attempt to lynch a prisoner. For some

Without Penalty J.B. Jones

reason, I began by researching that particular prisoner and let's just say...his story opened up a whole can of worms.

After the initial shock, I set out to learn as much about Sheriff Poag and his murder as possible from old newspapers and court records. The entire story is mind boggling to me. There is intrigue, politics, influential people, love, hate, deceit, etc. I have struggled exactly how to tell this story for a very long time. I certainly wanted to be extremely respectful to everyone that was involved in this tragedy. It is not my intention to bring shame on a family name or cause any embarrassment to my town or county. I simply wanted to share a interesting yet tragic story that happened long ago.

I hope that you enjoy this story as much as I have enjoyed researching and writing it.

Without Penalty — J.B. Jones

1

The Murder of Sheriff J.M. Poag

"Early this morning, one of the most daring and bloody assaults in the annals of the history of Tate County or the State of Mississippi was perpetrated at Senatobia, the county site..." *The Commercial Appeal; Memphis, Tennessee - Wednesday, April 12, 1905*

"One of the darkest and most deplorable crimes ever perpetrated in the county was committed here early Wednesday morning." *The Senatobia Democrat; Senatobia, Mississippi - April 14, 1905.*

"One of the most sensational affairs in the history of the state is enacted today." *Jackson Daily News; Jackson, Mississippi - Wednesday, April 12, 1905*

Without Penalty   J.B. Jones

The date was April 12, 1905. Sheriff John Macon Poag and his wife, Bessie were asleep in their room at the Tate County Jail when a noise outside jolted the couple awake. The sheriff immediately got out of bed to investigate the sound, but not before securing his pistol.

Once the sheriff entered the hallway, he heard a voice holler, "Oh...Johnny!" from outside the locked jailhouse doors.

Sheriff Poag answered, "Who's there?"

The voice responded, "It's me, Bob Pickle. Open up, I have a prisoner."

"I know Bob Pickle real well, and I feel very certain that you, sir, are not him."

"It's me, Sheriff. Open up!" the voice called out yet again.

Without Penalty   J.B. Jones

The sheriff relented, "Okay, I'll open the door to see what you want, but I know you are not who you say you are."

Upon turning the lock and lifting the bar securing the jailhouse doors, Sheriff Poag saw a crowd of masked men and a shotgun pointed towards him. He instinctively fired his pistol into the crowd and they instantly returned fire hitting Sheriff Poag. Sheriff Poag then fell to his knees and called out in agony, "I am murdered; I am shot twice." He staggered back into his room where his wife and children were screaming.

Sheriff Poag, his wife, Bessie and their five children were at the jail that fateful night. In addition to the sheriff's immediate family, his wife's brother, W.E. "Boss" Manahan was a special deputy and had stayed that night at the jail. Boss told reporters at the time that he had heard the commotion outside his door and arrived in time to witness a group of men running away. It was fortunate that he was there to help the sheriff. Boss was able to run

Without Penalty J.B. Jones

next door to the courthouse in an attempt to call for the doctor.

Unfortunately, he was unable to reach anyone by phone. Boss made the quick decision to go directly to the doctor's home down the street. Obviously, his actions and heroics that night helped sustain Sheriff Poag longer than I am sure anyone expected. As a result, the sheriff was able to describe his assailants, order bloodhounds to assist in the search for the masked men, and actually begin the investigation into his own murder.

Several local doctors responded to the call for help. Dr. Potter was the first to arrive followed by Dr. Ellis and Dr. Rosebourgh. The trio worked diligently on Sheriff Poag throughout the night. The sheriff had been shot in the right arm and the impact of the bullet had shattered the bone. He also had a gaping wound on his right side which quite possibly penetrated his lung. Poag told the doctors that he was confident he would die. The doctors advised him to rest and be quiet. However, the sheriff kept talking. Sheriff Poag apparently felt his last moments alive would be better spent telling everyone that would listen what had happened that night.

As the morning light began to shine throughout the jail, Sheriff John Macon Poag succumbed to his injuries and was pronounced dead at 6:45 a.m.

Word spread quickly across the country of the horrific events that had occurred in the early morning hours of April 12, 1905. Not only in Tate County, Mississippi, but all across the United States. Over the next few days, newspapers from New York to California reported on the murder of Sheriff John Macon Poag in Senatobia, Mississippi.

"Sheriff killed; shot by outlaws who sought to liberate a prisoner." The Roswell Daily Record; Roswell, New Mexico - April 12, 1905

"Sheriff gives up his life to save prisoner." The Piqua Daily Call; Piqua, Ohio - April 12, 1905

Without Penalty   J.B. Jones

"In the discharge of his duty, a Mississippi Officer sacrifices his life. The masqueraders demanded he release of a murderer and the Sheriff answered with bullets." The Charlotte News; Charlotte, North Carolina - April 12, 1905

"Mississippi Sheriff killed in the jail. Officer resists efforts to release a prisoner and is shot dead." San Francisco Chronicle; San Francisco, California - April 13, 1905

"Sheriff dies at his post." Roseburg Review; Roseburg, Oregon - April 13, 1905

"Masked men kill sheriff. He resisted their attempt to take a prisoner from jail." The Washington Post; Washington, DC - April 13, 1905

"Mob kills sheriff at jail. Dying man foils their plot to rescue prisoner." The New York Times; New York, New York - April 13, 1905

Over fifty newspapers in the United States and Canada reported on the murder of Sheriff Poag. The following list is only a few of

Without Penalty J.B. Jones

the many newspapers that ran the story throughout April:

News-Journal - Mansfield, Ohio
    Topeka State Journal - Topeka, Kansas
    The Minneapolis Journal - Minneapolis, Minnesota
    St. Louis Post-Dispatch - St. Louis, Missouri
    Racine Journal-Times - Racine, Wisconsin
    The News Journal - Wilmington, Delaware
    Evening Star - Washington, DC
    The Emporia Gazette - Emporia, Kansas
    The Fort Wayne Sentinel - Fort Wayne, Indiana
    Muskogee Times Democrat - Muskogee, Oklahoma
    The Daily Signal - Crowley, Louisiana
    The Butte Daily Post - Butte, Montana
    Reno Gazette-Journal - Reno, Nevada
    The Brooklyn Daily Eagle - Brooklyn, New York
    The Scranton Truth - Scranton, Pennsylvania

Without Penalty   J.B. Jones

      The Daily Review - Decanter, Illinois
      Bisbee Daily Review - Bisbee, Arizona
      The Tuscaloosa Times - Tuscaloosa, Alabama
      The Times Dispatch - Richmond, Virginia
      The Houston Post - Houston, Texas
      Pensacola News Journal - Pensacola, Florida
      Manitoba Morning Free Press - Winnipeg, Manitoba, Canada
      The Baltimore Sun - Baltimore, Maryland

This list could literally go on and on. I want to emphasis that the murder of Sheriff J.M. Poag was reported throughout the country in multiple states and Canada. This was big news in April 1905!

****

In my research, I found a several articles/letters written before this senseless murder. The first

Without Penalty J.B. Jones

article that I would like to share was written by the editor of the Senatobia Democrat when Mr. Poag announced his candidacy for sheriff:

John M. Poag for High Sheriff
 In this issue will be found the announcement of John M. Poag for the office of High Sheriff. Mr. Poag has served as deputy during the Brooks administration and is familiar with the duties connected with the position. His fitness for the office is well known to every voter hence it is useless to dwell here.
 Mr. Poag was reared and educated in the county and lived, prior to moving to Senatobia, at Thyatira. Personally he is a man of sterling qualities, high character, genial, and obliging. If the people favor him with the trust that he seeks he will make a good and faithful sheriff.

Poag was obviously well thought of throughout Tate County. He easily beat his opponents in the race for sheriff. In the primary election - August 1903, Poag received 965 votes - one of his opponents received 319 votes and the other 264 votes. After the election, Poag wrote the following letter that

Without Penalty — J.B. Jones

was published in the August, 21, 1903 edition of the Senatobia Democrat:

To my Fellow Countymen:

As I cannot see you individually and express my gratitude for the nomination of the important office of Sheriff of our county. I take this course to assure you that I hold keen appreciation for every vote cast for me and for the untiring efforts of my friends to mantle this important trust upon me. In return I assure you that my best efforts will be to give you an administration that will create harmony, good will and our general advancement.

To my former school pupils, I desire to state that it is most gratifying to me to know that you were active in bringing about my election and your interest will always stand most prominent in both my heart and mind during my life.

I have many friends in adjoining counties who were much interested in my candidacy and I wish to assure them of my full appreciation.

To the good ladies who extended hospitality to me at their homes, at picnics and used their influence for my election, I wish to assure that no one could be more grateful.

In conclusion, I desire to say that my opponents conducted their candidacies on a high plane and were at all times courteous and fair to me and our canvass began in friendship and ended likewise. It is a pleasure to make a canvass when you have gentlemen as opponents.
Yours most respectfully,
J.M. Poag

****

Sheriff John Macon Poag
>Born September 9, 1858
>Died April 12, 1905

Sheriff Poag had been married to his wife, Bessie Manahan Poag for 13 years and had five children - at the time of his death - their names and ages:
>Ruby Eugene Poag - 12 years old
>Mary Agnes Poag - 8 years old
>Bessie Lucille Poag - 5 years old
>Robert Macon Poag - 3 years old
>Mabel Poag - 11 months old

Without Penalty   J.B. Jones

Sheriff Poag is buried at Thyatria Cemetery in Thyatria, Mississippi. His monument is shared with Lizzie Aleine Poag, most likely his daughter who passed away in 1897. Unfortunately, his monument is not in the best condition especially considering this man died a hero in performance of his duty.

Final words...
One can only imagine the thoughts running through Sheriff Poag's mind as he made his way to the jailhouse doors. Not only did he swear to defend the prisoners at the jail, his entire family lived there. His bravery to defend the prisoners, and...essentially his home and family is unparalleled. The stand he took that night saved the life of his family, countless prisoners, and one man in particular - James Whitt. Whitt was the target of the mob and his story is unbelievable at best.

Sheriff Poag deserves to be remembered and honored...certainly not forgotten as it seems to me he has. His story needs to be told. I hope to do my best to share it with dignity and honor.

2

The Aftermath

As word of the murder of Sheriff J.M. Poag traveled across the country and Tate County, the small town of Senatobia was flooded with people from all sections of the county. In fact, The Senatobia Democrat reported that Sheriff Poag laid in state inside the jail where people by the hundreds came and grown men wept openly. Crowds gathered outside the courthouse trying to find out more information about what happened. Sheriff Poag was a beloved member of the community and people were highly inflamed upon hearing of his senseless murder.

The statements made by Sheriff Poag before his death helped launch the investigation. Leading the charge was Deputy Sheriff W.G.

Without Penalty J.B. Jones

"Willie" Lowery. Upon his arrival on the scene, Lowery searched the jail and documented the bullet holes around the porch and hall. He also found tracks outside in the yard which everyone involved was anxious to follow. The bloodhounds that Sheriff Poag had ordered earlier that morning were set to arrive on the noon train. Until then, everyone was left to speculate on who was responsible for such a brazen act.

The overall suspicion was that the mob was after a prisoner named James "Jim" Whitt. Whitt had killed a young man, O.R. "Buster" Thomason back in 1903. Whitt had been sentenced to hang by a jury in 1904, but the Mississippi Supreme Court had recently overturned his conviction and ordered a new trial. There had been rumors back in 1903 that a mob would try to lynch him to seek justice for the young man he killed. The rumors were rampant back in 1903 so much so that the sheriff at the time, B.B. Brooks had been advised to secretly move Jim Whitt to another county. Whitt was not brought back to Tate County until April 1904 to stand trial. After his conviction, thoughts of mob justice were no more.

However, when the Supreme Court handed down their decision and Whitt's arrived back in Senatobia, the rumors of a lynching began to circulate again. The court had advised Poag to be cautious. Which prompted Sheriff Poag to visit Buster Thomason's father, J. H. Thomason. Mr. Thomason had assured Poag that Whitt would not be harmed.

Interestingly enough, Sheriff Poag testified at the first trial of Jim Whitt in April 1904. He stated then that he had been advised since taking office to provide extra security for the prisoner. Poag told the court that he added more men than suggested to guard the jail. In addition, he asserted under oath the following: *"I am going to take all precautions necessary to prevent anything and I don't intend for anyone to be hanged here in this jail"*. Furthermore, Poag had been known to assert that any attempt to lynch a prisoner would be over his dead body. Even with the renewed threats in 1905, the sheriff continuously said that he would not tolerate such lawlessness in his jail.

As the investigation progressed, Sheriff Poag's deputies and other volunteers gathered at the jail to help - among them were John Bryant, W.H.D. McCants, Bob Pickle - a Constable from Arkabutla whose name the mob used to gain access to the jail, Button Graham, and John Whalen. John Whalen was reported to be an exceptional law man and was made the special detective. Deputy Lowery assembled a great team and put them to work immediately. In the meantime, according to newspaper reports, Governor James K. Vardaman had been apprised of the murder shortly before 10:00 a.m. that morning. He gave his full support and offered a reward of $500 to bring the group responsible to justice. Sheriff Poag was obviously well known and highly respected around the state capital.

As the noon hour approached, Deputy W.H.D. McCants and other eager citizens were sent to collect the dogs from the train station. Once the dogs arrived, a posse was formed and

Without Penalty   J.B. Jones

led by Lowery. The dogs picked up a scent immediately from the tracks at the jail. I am sure that not a single man in the group was surprised when the bloodhounds headed west. The group had to wonder if the rumors had been true and someone that was close to the murdered boy, Buster Thomason had killed Poag while seeking to lynch Jim Whitt. I am certain, however, that what happened next was not what they expected...

The bloodhounds took Deputy Lowery and his posse to Broom's gin. The dogs went right up to a group of horses hitched by the gin, but no one was found. The dogs continued onward leading the posse to Sam Howell's mill about 2 miles north of Strayhorn. Around the back of the mill was a makeshift camp. The posse found several men there and promptly arrested them without incident. The deputies searched the mill thoroughly. An overcoat with blood stains and hole that appeared to have been made by a bullet were found. Inside the coat pocket were several letters addressed to the owner of the mill - Sam Howell. Deputy Lowery found masks which provided further evidence that

Without Penalty   J.B. Jones

this group was involved in the murder of Sheriff Poag. According to the Senatobia Democrat, five men were arrested at the mill - Alex Nelson, Henry Hunter, John Tully, John Boling, Rose Beech and Tobe Williams. However, the owner of the overcoat, Sam Howell was not at the mill. The posse assumed from the blood and hole in the coat that Sam Howell had been shot by Sheriff Poag. A woman working at a home near the mill confirmed that Howell was wounded, but she did not know how. The men arrested would not disclose any information and not one of the men questioned why the posse was there or why they were being arrested.

At some point between Wednesday, April 12 and Thursday, April 13, J.T. Gabbert was appointed acting sheriff. Mr. Gabbert was a local businessman in Senatobia. I am not sure exactly who appointed him, but his leadership was needed to deal with the fallout to come. Before noon on Thursday, April 13, Norman Clayton, the son of the former state representative, S.T. Clayton, had sent word that he was to surrender. When Clayton arrived, he reportedly made a full confession

Without Penalty J.B. Jones

naming everyone involved in the mob. Upon hearing the confession, acting Sheriff Gabbert and his deputies quietly gathered together and deputized 15 additional men. Warrants were issued and shortly after 1:00 p.m. a heavily armed posse headed west towards Strayhorn. The posse divided in squads and split up searching for the mob. About 7 miles west of Senatobia, several men left the road and arrested Tate McConnell at his plow handle. In addition, John Butler, Willie Sinquefield, O.L. Manning and J.H. Thomason were all arrested while working in the fields. As these men were being brought to Senatobia, another posse continued the search for the other men implicated by Clayton.

J.H. Thomason, the father of Buster Thomason (the young man Jim Whitt killed) confessed to being the leader of the mob. He said he wanted vengeance for his son. One newspaper made the assertion that Thomason was on the verge of a mental breakdown. Not only was J.H. Thomason, the father of the murdered boy, he was the Tate County Supervisor for District 1 which made him a rather well-known and prominent figure in the

Without Penalty   J.B. Jones

county. Thankfully, Thomason was forth coming and expressed regret for the death of Sheriff Poag. He stated that Alex Nelson (one of the men arrested at the mill) fired the fatal shot that killed the sheriff. Thomason named other participants in the mob including the Spencer brothers and Dave Smith. He also exonerated a few men that had been arrested earlier. All together 13 men were charged in the murder of Sheriff J.M. Poag.

Governor Vardaman continued to closely follow the investigation. He ordered that Jim Whitt be sent to Jackson until his trial began. The governor also spoke harshly about the perpetrators of this crime in the Vicksburg Evening Post; Vicksburg, Mississippi - Friday, April 14, 1905 - *"I think that the killing of Sheriff Poag was a most brutal and cowardly assassination of a faithful and efficient officer whose fidelity to duty sets an example that is worthy of being emulated by all the law officers of the State of Mississippi. There is one lesson that should not be forgotten by the men who are charged with the enforcement of the law and that is that when a man or a dozen men undertake to override the law, and*

Without Penalty   J.B. Jones

interfere with an officer in the performance of his duty, the proper thing for him to do is to shoot straight, instead of over the head of the offending party. If Mr. Poag had done that the cowardly scoundrel who took his life would have been put in the grave instead of Poag. If it is known that the officer is going to do his duty and shoot when necessary, there is no danger of a mob trying to take his prisoner from him. Every possible effort will be made to punish the men who are responsible for this outrage. All the power invested in the governor of the State of Mississippi will be employed to bring these assassins to justice."

Subsequently, Vardaman appointed a special prosecutor to handle to case, Mr. J.F. Dean. Mr. Dean along with Acting Sheriff, J.T. Gabbert made the following statements in the April 21, 1905 edition of the Senatobia Democrat:

"We have ten men in jail. There were thirteen men in the mob that murdered Sheriff Poag at the jail Wednesday morning, and we have all, but three of them who are now at large. Eight of the ten men confessed that they were members of the mob and gave the names of the other five. The statements made by the eight men agree in almost every detail.

Without Penalty — J.B. Jones

They said three men were left to hold the horses, while the ten went to the jail." J.T. Gabbert

J.F. Dean, the special prosecutor, made these remarks. *"These confessions were made by the prisoners voluntarily. They were not urged. There was no extortion whatsoever and no promises of any kind were made to them. Each of these confessions was taken in the hearing of at least two reputable citizens besides myself and were taken separately. The prisoners corroborated each other's statement in almost every detail. Six of the ten men have been sent away. We sent these men to other prisons, not from fear of any mob violence, either for or against them. We did not fear that they would be taken out and murdered by the friends of Mr. Poag, nor did we fear that they would be liberated by their own friends. They were removed, first, because of the crowded condition of the jail, and second, because we thought it absolutely essential to separate them and keep them from communicating with each other and with others until we could get all the information they possessed. In addition to the confession of the men, there is full and complete proof of their guilt and sufficient evidence to secure a conviction of not only the ones we have arrested, but of those to be arrested, aside from their confession, we believe firmly we can convict the entire thirteen of murder. The confession of the eight men show that J.H. Thomason, the father of Buster Thomason, who was killed by Jim Whitt, was the leader of the mob. The twelve men who assisted him were Sam Howell, Norman Clayton, Tate McConnell, Henry Hunter, Alex Nelson, Dave Smith, Will Sinquefield, O.L. Manning, Tom Vincent, William Still and Jack and Preston Spencer. Thomason, Howell, Clayton, and Mcconnell are now in the jail at Hernando, Alex Nelson and Henry Hunter are at Batesville and Tom Vincent, O.L. Manning, Will Sinquefield, and Dave Smith are at Senatobia. William Still and Jack and Preston Spencer are still at large, but will no doubt be captured within the next few days. The citizens of Senatobia and the county have done some commendable work in detecting those alleged to be responsible for the death of Sheriff Poag."*

****

In the days and weeks after the murder,

several newspapers published tributes in honor of J.M. Poag.

Published in the Senatobia Democrat - Special to the Commercial Appeal
>Washington, April 14
>*The tragedy at Senatobia, Mississippi on the morning of April 12 in which Sheriff J.M. Poag lost his life in the defense of a prisoner against a mob, has attracted a good deal of comment in the East. Leading newspapers like the New York Times urge the erection of a monument to commemorate the courage of the martyred Sheriff. The Times says: "The people of Senatobia, Mississippi will fall in their duty as men and as citizens if they do not erect a monument to commemorate the courage and the civic virtue of J.M. Poag, late sheriff of Tate County who was shot and killed while attempting to defend a prisoner against a mob that had attacked the jail with the intention of lynching him. Sheriff Poag's example is of priceless value and his blood has be shed upon Southern soil, where Sheriffs are, perhaps, more frequently than elsewhere called upon to confront such perils as these which have cost him his life. The Southerners are a brave*

people. Sheriff Poag was a brave man. They ought to honor him and keep his memory green.

Published in the August 25, 1905 edition of the Senatobia Democrat:

In Memory of John M. Poag

The subject of this tribute was a man and a mason. Need we say more? The night of April 12, 1905 will ever be memorable in the history of Tate County. On that fateful night as our beloved brother lay slumbering in the repose of well-earned rest, feeling that sense of security that is the birthright of every law-abiding citizen; surrounded by his own loved ones who dreamed of naught but pleasure; at that hour when sleep is deepest and sweetest, he was called upon to stand between a mob on the one hand, thirsting for blood, and the prison cells above, in which reposed a man once adjudged unworthy even to live, whose hands were gory with human blood. Will John Poag make a feint and then with pretended reluctance turn over the prison keys or will he not? This question was pondered well by the mob and doubtless answered in the affirmative. But a man of mob nature and temperament cannot judge correctly the courses and conduct of one of nature's nobleman and hence they easily mistook a man and his devotion to duty which impelled him to fire the signal of his own death.

The mob fled in confusion and our martyr sheriff staggered back into his room to expire with the night that had passed thus far so sweetly.

No braver, truer, or more self-sacrificing man ever lived than John M. Poag.

Therefore, Resolved, that we tender to his bereaved family our expressions of deepest sympathy and condolence with assurance of our personal interest in their future welfare.

Hall of Solomon Lodge, No 126, Independence, Mississippi, May 27, 1905

T.C. Newsom
F.M. Davis
J.S. Russwurm

In the April 21, 1905 edition of the Senatobia Democrat, this story was published about a meeting held at the courthouse.

To Erect Home

Meeting held Wednesday - Another Meeting will be held next Monday.

A mass meeting was held at the courthouse Wednesday for the purpose of raising money to

Without Penalty   J.B. Jones

erect a home for Mrs. J.M. Poag and children. The home will stand as a monument to our late sheriff, who laid down his life in the discharge of duty. On motion of J.T. Gabbert, J.A. Wooten was elected chairman and R.C. Smith, secretary. H.I. Gill presented the purpose of the meeting after which he introduced the following resolution which was adopted.

"Whereas, our community, state and country realize its great obligations to the late J.M. Poag who so bravely laid down his life in the discharge of his duty as Sheriff of Tate County on the morning of April 12th, and whereas, as citizens we are anxious in some measure to show our appreciation of this high performance of duty,

Therefore, be it resolved that we as citizens in mass meeting assembled, do select a committee of three citizens to receive and receipt for popular subscriptions to fund of $2500 to $3000 for the purpose of buying Mrs. Poag and her five fatherless children a home in Senatobia, Mississsippi or other place in Tate County as will be satisfactory to Mrs. Poag, that she may be of us and that her children may grow up to be educated in our midst.

Without Penalty   J.B. Jones

Resolved further that J.T. Gabbert, W.B. Roseborourgh, and H.I. Gill constitute said committee to receive and receipt for said subscription to invest said funds when collected in a home.

On motion B.A. Tucker requested that his name be omitted from the above resolution and H.I. Gill's be inserted as a member of the committee. Carried.

B.A. Tucker introduced the following explanatory resolution, which was unanimously adopted.

Resolved, that we deplore the fact that mob violence has asserted itself in our county, and that we feel keenly the disgrace, humiliation and reproach cast upon our county and ourselves as its citizens by the death of our brave and devoted Sheriff J.M. Poag at the hands of a mob.

Resolved, that while as a reading and intelligent people we appreciate the value of daily newspapers, we deplore the fact that the daily papers which circulate in this community have seen it to publish unfounded and sensational reports of the condition of affairs existing in this county.

Resolved, that we denounce as untrue and as pure yellow journalism the reports that the men arrested for the murder of Sheriff Poag are now or have been in any danger of mob violence themselves or that any feud or ill feeling exists between the eastern and western parts of Tate County, or between the citizens of Senatobia and the citizens of any other part of the county or that militia will be needed to preserve order at our court. And we assert that all such statements are the creations of the imagination of sensational and irresponsible newspaper reporters and do not exist in fact.

J.F. Dean offered a resolution that court adjourn one hour Monday out of respect to the memory of J.M. Poag and that a meeting be held during the hour at the courthouse by the citizens of the county. Honorable W.J. East was appointed a committee of one to make all necessary arrangements for this meeting.

The subscription list was opened and the following donations were made:
Senatobia Bank - $50.00
Tucker & Gabbert - $25.00
Garrott & Co. - $25.00
R.E. Walker - $10.00
J.T. Gabbert & Co. - $25.00
J.F. Dean - $5.00

Without Penalty J.B. Jones

H.I. Gill - $20.00
J.A. Wooten - $20.00
J.R. Solomon - $5.00
W.T. Wright - $2.50
J.L. Friedheim - $2.50
C.P. Varner - $3.00
A.L. Kerr - $2.50
J.H. Bernard - $10.00
J.S. Bowen - $10.00
Phil A. Rush - $10.00
M.H. Thompson - $5.00
R.C. Smith - $5.00
Walker Wood - $5.00
J.M. Salmon - $1.00
Total = $240.00

Governor Vardaman's words sent by telegram directly to Mrs. Poag that were published in the Jackson Daily News; Jackson, Mississippi on April 12, 1905:

Accept my heartfelt sympathy and condolence in this the darkest hour of your life. While I know that words are vain and meaningless to a heart distressed as yours must be, I have this consolation to offer: your husband died nobly at the post of duty, and the world is better for him having live. May God's tender mercy and His all-enveloping love sustain you. J.K. Vardaman, Governor

3

The Mob Trials: Arraignment

On Monday, April 17, 1905, roughly five days after the murder of Sheriff J.M. Poag, the spring term of the Tate County Circuit Court began. Due to the magnitude of recent events, Judge J.B. Boothe wasted no time in selecting the grand jury and informing them of their duties.

Because of the excitement surrounding the sheriff's murder and the second trial of James "Jim" Whitt, there was an unprecedented number of spectators in the courtroom. I can only imagine that it was clear to everyone that this session would be like no other. As a result, I feel certain that Judge Boothe seized this opportunity to address the audience and grand jury. His eloquent speech

Without Penalty — J.B. Jones

was published in the April 24, 1905 edition of the Senatobia Democrat:

"I am not here to eulogize J.M. Poag. He needs no eulogy from me here. A sheriff has been shot down. There are eight sheriffs in the district: there are none whom the court could more implicitly rely on than Mr. Poag. He has been stricken down - by whom the court does not know. It is your duty to find out. His death is the natural outcome of mob violence and unless this is checked your children and my children will become its victims. You let your children see these ghastly crimes and believe them to be right and just, and soon neighbors will array themselves against neighbor. If you teach your boys that they may take the execution of the law in their own hands, you had as well tear down your courthouse. If this madness is allowed to go on, Breathitt County, Kentucky will be regarded as a haven of refuge compared to Tate County, Mississippi. Unless you keep this oath inviolate you will call down the maledictions of the great and just God. Unless you pause and consider, unless this course is checked. Tate county and this grand state of Mississippi will soon be rife with evil feuds and brothers will shed brothers' blood. If a conspiracy is formed to violate the law

and in this attempt an innocent man is killed, the man who did the shooting is a murderer, the accessories are none the less murderers, and all engaged in the conspiracy are guilty of murder. This is the law in Mississippi."

The powerful message heard in the courtroom was needed that day and no one was better to deliver it than the unassuming judge whose *"armless sleeve attested to his own valor as a solider."* Judge Boothe obviously regarded Sheriff J.M. Poag with the same honor as a fallen comrade.

On Monday, May 1, 1905, the eleven men charged with the murder of Sheriff Poag were arraigned. The crowd was the largest seen in years at the Tate County courthouse. People from all over Tate County came to witness this important event. The May 3, 1905 edition of the Senatobia Democrat reported that *"perhaps never in the history of the state were eleven men brought before the bar of justice charged with murder of the same man."* J.H. Thomason, Tate McConnell, Sam Howell, Tom Vincent, Alex

Without Penalty   J.B. Jones

Nelson, Henry Hunter, Will Sinquefield, Oscar Manning, Dave Smith, William Still, and Norman Clayton stood before the court to answer for the indictments brought against them. All eleven of the men plead not guilty.

The defense attorneys were J.H. Farley, R.E.L. Morgan of Hernando and J.W. Lauderdale. District Attorney W.A. Roane and J.F. Dean appeared for the state.

After the defendants' plea, the defense made the request for a change of venue. The prosecution offered no objection. However, the state had one stipulation that no one county would be burdened.

After making this request, Judge Boothe *"made a thorough investigation as to whether the court had the power to perform such a distribution of the cases."* Obviously, this was new territory for the judge. After careful consideration, Judge Boothe made the following ruling to distribute the defendants:

Holly Springs, Marshall County - J.H. Thomason, R.T. McConnell, Sam Howell, and Tom Vincent

Without Penalty J.B. Jones

Oxford, Lafayette County - Alex Nelson, Henry Hunter, Will Sinquefield, and Oscar Manning

Batesville, Panola County - Dave Smith, William Still, and Norman Clayton.

Several of these men were dispersed to different jails across Northwest Mississippi to alleviate crowding in the Tate County jail while awaiting trial. I love the statements made in the May 3, 1905 - Senatobia Democrat about the crowd control at the jail, *"The capacity of the little jail that stands west of the courthouse has been tested during the week. There have been more than 20 prisoners confined within the walls. Sheriff Lowery remains careful. No apprehension has been felt on the part of the officers that the unexpected might happen, but in order to be on the safe side every precaution has been taken to prevent any further history in connection with our now famous "lock-up" Every night a strong force of officers has been stationed at the jail."*

The first of the three mob trials began on September 1, 1905 in Holly Springs - Marshall

Without Penalty   J.B. Jones

County, Mississippi.

Statements in italics/quotations were taken directly from the May 3, 1905 edition of the Senatobia Democrat.

There are several interesting people involved in this story. Being the nerd I am, I tried to find out as much as possible about each one. In fact, I can most likely tell you where everyone is buried and I have probably visited their graves! After I read Judge J.B. Boothe's speech featured above, I wanted to know more about him. The following is a short synopsis of his life:

James Benjamin Boothe was born in Gates County, North Carolina on March 1, 1844. When he was very small, his parents moved to Mississippi. In 1861, Boothe entered the Southern army. He was involved in several battles in Virginia and lost his right arm in the battle of the Wilderness. When he returned home to Mississippi, Boothe taught

Without Penalty   J.B. Jones

school before being admitted to the bar and eventually practicing law. Around 1874, J.B. Boothe moved to Sardis where he became interested in politics. He served as State Senator from 1886 to 1890. After serving in the senate, Boothe practiced law in Sardis and was made circuit judge in 1903. In 1907, he either retired or did not seek reappointment as circuit judge. Boothe died on February 8, 1932 in Lexington County, Mississippi.

4

The Murder of O.R. "Buster" Thomason

Sheriff Poag was killed because a mob wanted to lynch a man named James "Jim" Whitt. In order to fully understand what happened to the sheriff, it is important to know who James Whitt was and how he happened to be in the Tate County jail on the morning of April 12, 1905.

The date was December 24, 1903. The day started off like any other in the Strayhorn community. Excitement was in the air because after all it was Christmas Eve. A young man named O. R. "Buster" Thomason along with his friends, Henry Wilson, Alex Nelson, and Charlie Rochelle decided to head over to Bill Scroggins' house early that morning for a

Without Penalty J.B. Jones

hunt. Once the group arrived, another man named James "Jim" Whitt came up with his gun looking to join them on the hunt. Bill Scroggins asked the group to join him in drinking a dram of whiskey. After the drink, there are differing accounts of what happened next...

    The best I can piece together is that Buster Thomason made a comment about Jim Whitt's family specifically his wife. The comment made Jim Whitt very angry. According to Thomason's friends, Jim wanted to play a gambling game called crackaloo*, but Buster declined. Buster reportedly said that he had too much respect for Mrs. Scroggins, Whitt, his wife, and family to play such a game in their presence. At that statement, Whitt allegedly got out his knife and said, "What did you say about my wife" and the two commenced to fighting. After the fuss, the two men went their separate ways until running into each other late that afternoon. Whitt tells a different story about what was said, but I'll save that for another time...Regardless of the reasons and what was said, everyone involved

Without Penalty J.B. Jones

admitted that Jim Whitt and Buster Thomason had a rather heated argument that morning.

Later that afternoon, around 4:00 p.m., Charlie Rochelle, Henry Wilson, and Buster Thomason were riding on the "big" road to a Christmas tree in Strayhorn. The trio were headed south when they met Jim Whitt walking towards them with his gun. Supposedly, Charlie Rochelle encountered Whitt first. Whitt asked for his knife back and Rochelle complied. Rochelle continued south and rode only a short distance before hearing a gun shot. According to who you want to believe, there are several different versions of the exchange between Whitt and Thomason. Despite what was said, Buster Thomason got off his mule to face Whitt. Once he was down, Whitt immediately shot Thomason hitting his left arm. Thomason grabbed his left arm, turned, and proceeded to walk off when Whitt shot again. The second shot hit Thomason in the back and he immediately fell. Whitt unbreeched his gun, put two shells back in the gun, and walked on heading north to his home where he met Representative S.T. Clayton and his daughter Belle.

Without Penalty J.B. Jones

The particulars of what was said and who said it are unsubstantiated at best. Anytime you have multiple witnesses, you will have multiple stories. One thing that can be proven is that James Whitt shot Buster Thomason two times - one shot...broke his left arm and the second shot hit him in the back. Why or how this happened? Well, that is another story altogether...a different reason or story from everyone involved.

James Whitt turned himself to Sheriff B.B. Brooks on the night of December 24, 1903. Based on advice from the court and rumors of a possible lynching, Whitt was secretly moved to Batesville on Christmas day. He remained in Batesville until April 1904. At that time, he was brought back to Senatobia to stand trial for the murder of O.R. Thomason.

*Crackaloo - A gambling game which players throw coins at the ceiling aiming to have them fall as near as possible to a certain crack in the floor.

5

The 1904 Trial of James "Jim" Whitt

April 1904
State of Mississippi vs James "Jim" Whitt
Case #1773

> Judge - J.A. Boothe
> Prosecution - W.A. Roane

Jim Whitt was arraigned on **April 28, 1904** for the murder of O.R. "Buster" Thomason. He pleaded not guilty.

Due to Whitt's lack of funds or support, he was unable to hire an attorney until roughly a week before trial. The attorney was Leland L. Pearson from Batesville. Pearson was apparently reluctant to take the case, but out of pity for Whitt's circumstances agreed. He began Whitt's defense by requesting a continuance until the next term. Pearson filed a rather lengthy and detailed affidavit. The argument was that Whitt had been unable to secure an attorney or conduct any investigation into his case. Furthermore, Whitt was in need to speak to his brother. His brother had traveled from Tennessee and spoke to several people in the Strayhorn community. The information that he collected was argued to be vital to Whitt's defense. Unfortunately, Whitt's brother had returned to Tennessee and due to lack of funds could not return until later in the year.

However, Judge J.A. Boothe denied the request for a continuance.

After failing to move the court to grant a continuance, Pearson filed a motion for a change of venue based on the belief that the public sentiment was very strong against Whitt. Several witnesses were then called to testify whether they felt Whitt could get a fair trial in Tate County. Former Sheriff B.B. Brooks testified about his reasons for moving Whitt to Batesville. Under oath, the former sheriff stated that he was "*advised by people from Strayhorn and the court*". Brooks had contacted Judge Boothe after Thomason was killed and informed the judge of hearing rumors of violence against Whitt. As a result, Judge Boothe told Brooks, "*not take any chances*". Pearson also questioned Sheriff J.M. Poag and other members of the community hoping to prove that his client was indeed a hated man.

After hearing all the testimony, Judge Boothe ruled against the change of venue and Sheriff Poag was ordered to draw a special venire (jury list) of 50 potential jurors. When the judge ruled against the requested motions, Leland Pearson withdrew from the case. Obviously, Pearson must have felt like he could not win. As a result, the court appointed S.W. Jones, George Lindsey, and W.J. East to be Whitt's attorneys.

When the new attorneys took over Whitt's case, the trio immediately filed for a continuance. One of the multitude of reasons stated in the motion was that a witness could not be located named Wat Luckett. Mr. Luckett had allegedly witnessed the killing of Buster Thomason. In addition, Whitt had also obtained the names of two other witnesses that could help in his defense. Apparently, these two additional witnesses were not available at this time. Upon reviewing the brief submitted, the court overruled the motion for a continuance.

Whitt's attorneys were not finished. They quickly moved the court to quash and set aside the jury list. The allegation set forth in this motion basically indicated that J.H. Thomason manipulated the jury list and placed the names that he wanted to serve on the jury without regard for the law. The defense counsel went as far as to call the circuit clerk to testify to how the jury was selected and drawn. Upon hearing this testimony, Judge Boothe apparently felt that there was enough evidence without going any further to quash the jury pool (venire) and directed the clerk to issue a special venire to the sheriff to summon 30 men to appear for jury service.

W.J. East continued to spend the morning entering multiple motions including one to quash the grand jury on the same grounds as mentioned earlier. He also made a motion to quash the indictment. Of course,

Without Penalty J.B. Jones

Judge Boothe overruled those requests. East was relentless and continued to file motions including one asking for an extra day to review the jury list. Judge Boothe ultimately answered with "I would like to go on with this case, gentlemen" to which the case finally proceeded.

May 5, 1904
Jury sworn and trial of Jim Whitt officially began...

The state began the trial by calling Buster Thomason's friends - Henry Wilson and Charlie Rochelle. The two told basically the same story of what happened on Christmas Eve when Jim Whitt shot Buster. According to the Wilson and Rochelle, the three men were approximately one mile from Buster's home heading to a Christmas tree festival when they ran into Jim Whitt walking along with his gun. They asked Whitt to join them, but he declined. Instead, Whitt asked Charlie Rochelle for his knife. Rochelle gave Whitt his knife back and rode on past him.

The trouble began when Whitt and Buster met.

Without Penalty   J.B. Jones

According to Wilson, Whitt stopped Buster and said, "*hold on, Buster, they tell me we like to have had a fight this morning, how about it?*"

Buster responded, "*No, there ain't nothing to it - you have been a little mad at me, but I haven't got a thing in the world against you.*"

Whitt demanded, "*you get down and tell me about it.*"

As Buster was getting down off his mule, Whitt raised his gun and shot hitting Buster in the left arm. Buster turned around holding his arm and walked off, but Whitt shot him again in the back.

Apparently earlier that morning at Mr. Scroggins' home, Buster and Whitt had a rather heated argument. Henry Wilson and Charlie Rochelle both testified that the cause of this particular argument was due to comments that Buster made about Whitt's wife. According to Wilson, Whitt even said later in the day that he wanted to put two shots in Buster before night.

Mrs. Belle Brown (formerly Belle Clayton) was called to testify because Belle and her father, S.T. Clayton had witnessed the shooting. Unfortunately, S.T. Clayton had passed away in February 1904. Belle recalled that they were traveling south about 30 yards from the shooting heading directly towards the scene. She stated that 3 boys were riding together in the road. Belle noticed that one man got down off his mule and about the time he got down - the first shot was fired. The man stopped and grabbed his arm, ran off, and another man stepped around the mule to shoot again. Belle was certain that the man who was shot had his back to the other man. As they got closer, the man shooting (James Whitt) turned around, unbreeched his gun, put two shells in and met S.T. and Belle Clayton on the road. Upon meeting the Clayton's, Belle said that Whitt said, "*Good evening, Mr. Clayton*" and walked off. Interestingly, Belle testified that she did not see anyone else around besides Henry Wilson, Charlie Rochelle, Buster Thomason, and James Whitt.

After hearing Belle Clayton's testimony, the state called Jim Whitt's father-in-law, J.J. Morris. He stated that Whitt had asked to borrow his gun that morning at breakfast to go on a hunt. Of course, Mr. Morris allowed Whitt to take the gun. Unfortunately, Whitt used the gun to kill Buster Thomason that night.

    Mr. Morris testified that Alex Nelson and Bill Scroggins had told about the argument between Whitt and Buster. After hearing about the trouble, Mr. Morris said he was concerned especially when Whitt came home around dinner that day. After Whitt left, Mr. Morris found his daughter crying which prompted him to go out to look for Jim Whitt. He found Whitt at Mr. Kizer's home and told Whitt to come home because Louisa, Whitt's wife, was upset. Whitt then told Mr. Morris that, *"Buster has got to take back what he said. He has talked about your family and Mr. Kizer's family."* This prompted the attorney to ask about Louisa and Jim's marriage. Morris felt that the couple got along reasonably well during their time together. However, Mr. Morris did not want Louisa to visit Jim in jail because she had told her father that Whitt had a living wife in Alabama... (This bombshell was not explained any further - the defense obviously objected to the statement by Mr. Morris and there is no mention of it again...)

Without Penalty J.B. Jones

Other witnesses testified to hearing Whitt say that Buster had been talking about his folks and he couldn't stand it. Whitt even told his brother-in-law that he was going to kill Buster before the sun went down. However, the defense through cross-examination tried to paint a different picture of Buster Thomason. Mr. East, one of Whitt's attorney, asked the various witnesses about Buster telling multiple people that he had been having a good time with all the women on Chigger Ridge - which included Jim's wife and other young ladies. The defense was determined to attack the character of Buster Thomason. With each witness called, the question was repeatedly asked about Buster breaking up a marriage and at another time a girl at the altar. It was clear that the defense wanted to portray Buster Thomason as a womanizer that had destroyed at least one marriage. However, the district attorney objected to every question that mentioned a particular woman. Witness after witness was asked questions like, "*Did Buster Thomason fool a woman and backed out of marrying her*"; "*Did Buster Thomason cause the separation between*

Without Penalty   J.B. Jones

Ernest McIver and his wife?"; Did you ever hear of Buster Thomason remark about Mrs. McIver?" and on and on.

Surprisingly, Jim Whitt took the stand in his own defense. He began his testimony by giving a detailed description of where he had been since December 25, 1903. Being in Batesville all that time, Jim said that no family had been able to visit him. Whitt was asked about his relationship with his wife, he said, *"they got along splendidly"*. His wife had written him letters and seemed like she was alright. According to Whitt, the trouble with Buster had begun on the Sunday before Christmas 1903. Whitt's story was that Buster had come over to Mr. Morris' house to visit. Whitt and Buster were talking when Buster spoke some words that Whitt did not like. Buster had made some remarks about Mr. Kizer's daughter and implicated Whitt's wife, Louisa. Buster told Whitt *"that he had a good time with all the girls up and down that ridge."* Whitt was very angry, but was not able to say anything to Buster at that time. He did not see Buster again until Christmas Eve.

Without Penalty — J.B. Jones

Whitt's version of the fuss at Mr. Scroggins' house on Christmas Eve is slightly different than previous testimony. He asserted that Alex Nelson, Charlie Rochelle, Henry Wilson, Buster Thomason, and Bill Scroggins were all by the barn. Whitt decided at that time to speak to Buster about the remarks that he had made the week before by saying "*I would be glad if you wouldn't make such remarks about the women on that road because I married one of them and I thought she was a nice lady.*"

Buster responded with, "*The very idea, you must be jealous.*" Whitt said that Buster kept on until the two began fighting. Whitt said he gave Charlie Rochelle his knife because the group thought he was going to cut Buster.

According to his testimony, Whitt admitted to drinking a good bit throughout the day, but denied ever being drunk. In detailing how Buster was killed, Whitt said he was walking home to Mr. Morris' house when he saw Charlie, Henry, and Buster coming towards him. Whitt's exact words were "*they came up abreast like*", but Charlie stopped and got his knife back. Buster stopped next and said, "*we had a fuss this morning and we've got to*

Without Penalty J.B. Jones

settle it." Whitt said that Buster got off his mule and attempted to get his gun because Buster had his hand in his pocket. Fearing for his life, Whitt shot Buster as quick as he could because he knew Buster generally carried a pistol.

After Jim Whitt's testimony, the case was handed over to the jury.

The next day, May 6, 1904, the jury returned with a guilty verdict - murder in the first degree. James "Jim" Whitt was sentenced to hang on June 10, 1904. However, the defense quickly filed a motion to set aside the verdict to which Judge J.B. Boothe overruled.

When the defense attorneys failed to get a new trial for Whitt, they appealed to the Mississippi Supreme Court on May 20, 1904. This action allowed Jim Whitt to remain in the Panola County jail until the appeal could be heard effectively keeping him from the gallows.

The case of James Whitt v. State of Mississippi was finally argued and decided in the Mississippi Supreme Court in February 1905. W.J. East, S.W. Jones, and G.W. Lindsey argued that James Whitt was "*erroneously denied a continuation by the court*". The case was featured in the eBook, "<u>Cases Argued and Decided in Supreme Court of Mississippi, Volume 85</u>". The decision taken directly from this book is as follows:

> *The supreme court, on appeal in a criminal case, in passing upon the action of the trial court in denying a continuance, is confined to the record and cannot consider a certified copy of a subpoena issued for a witness nor an affidavit averring that he was present in court during the trial of the case, such papers not having been of record in court below at the time of trial.*
>
> *C.J. Whitfield delivered the opinion of the court. The second application for a continuance should have been granted on the showing made by this record. The attorney-general, realizing this, has had filed here a certified copy of the original subpoena by Wat Luckett, showing that the subpoena was issued and executed May 4th, and an affidavit of the sheriff to the effect that the witness was present in court during the whole trial. But these papers were obtained after the adjournment of the court, and are not a part of this record, and cannot be looked to by us. If the original subpoena*

Without Penalty   J.B. Jones

was on file when this application was made, the witness was in attendance, it would have been easy to show these facts in answer to the application; but no showing was made, so far as the record discloses. The twenty-sixth section of article three of the constitution, and the decisions thereunder, make reversal imperative. Reversed and remanded.

The Vicksburg Evening Post; Vicksburg, Mississippi - Wednesday, February 1, 1905 reported this decision in simpler terms: *In the case of Whitt vs. State, a death sentence case, the court held that the lower court erred in not granting a continuance asked for on the ground of absence of witnesses.* As a result of this decision, Jim Whitt was granted a new trial.

After the Mississippi Supreme Court decision, Jim Whitt was brought back to the Tate County jail in April 1905 for the spring term of the Tate County Circuit Court. Obviously, we know the outcome of this move back to Tate County.

6

The 1905 Trial of James "Jim" Whitt

April, 1905
State of Mississippi vs. James "Jim" Whitt
Case #1773

>Judge - J.B. Boothe
>Prosecution - W.A. Roane

After the members of the mob were granted a change of venue and the court dates set for later in the year, the spring term of the Tate County circuit court continued with the second trial of James "Jim" Whitt.

On April 24, 1905, the case began with virtually the same witnesses from the first trial. Henry Wilson was the first to take the stand for the state. District Attorney W.A. Roane once again began by asking Wilson to

Without Penalty   J.B. Jones

tell the story of the fight between Buster and Jim. Then, Roane proceeded to get Wilson to describe the shooting. Wilson's stories had not changed from the first trial. However, the cross-examination from the defense became heated. Mr. East, Whitt's attorney, was relentless in his attacks on the integrity of not only Henry Wilson, but Buster Thomason. Questions ranged from - whether Buster had a gun on him at all times; to whether the group including Wilson was extremely drunk the day of the shooting. East continued with the accusations that Wilson had been a part of a plot to kill Whitt after the fight between Whitt and Buster. Wilson was asked whether he took a gun off of Buster after the shooting....and much more. It was obvious that the defense wanted to discredit Henry Wilson by this particular line of questioning...at the very least plant seed of doubt in the minds of the jury.

Mrs. Belle Brown repeated the same story as before. Interestingly, Belle said in her testimony this go around that her first thought when she saw the shooting was that the victim, Buster might be her brother, Norman.

Without Penalty   J.B. Jones

The exchange between Belle and S.W. Jones, one of the defense attorneys is priceless to me. It just so happens that Belle Brown was my husband's great-grandmother and proved herself to be quite feisty. When asked about her brother Norman, Belle said "*he's in jail*". The questioning continued by the attorney asking why Norman was in jail and she responded that "*he was awaiting tria*l then Belle blurted out "*Does that concern this case any?*"

This frustrated response from Belle prompted Roane to object and Judge Boothe said, "*I can't think of nothing in the world you could ask about her brother that would be material to this case. It's totally immaterial where he is.*"

After Judge Boothe's statement, Roane withdrew his objection and Mr. Jones told Belle to answer his question.

Belle said, "*I haven't heard any question, yet.*"

"*Is your brother indicted for killing J.M. Poag?*"

She answered, "*he's supposed to be. I don't know anything about it.*"

Without Penalty   J.B. Jones

Norman Clayton, Belle Brown's brother, was actually part of the mob that killed Sheriff Poag and was in jail awaiting his trial.

The defense's case was centered around discrediting the state's witnesses and Buster Thomason. They called several witnesses to attest to Buster Thomason's propensity for violence with several stating that Buster had a bad reputation for truth and veracity. In fact, another witness stated that the reason behind the killing was a woman.

In addition, Wat Luckett, the witness that was allegedly not been present at the 1904 trial and the reason that the supreme court granted a new trial, testified to witnessing the shooting. He said that Henry Wilson and Charlie Rochelle were riding ahead of Buster and could not have seen the actual shots fired.

The biggest surprise of this trial was the testimony of Jim Whitt. His story changed... especially about his wife. In the previous trial, he said they got along splendidly; this time around he said his marriage was tolerable. Whitt painted a completely different picture of his wife and Buster Thomason. Even testifying

Without Penalty J.B. Jones

that the reason he went to Alabama in the fall of 1902 was because of Buster being too intimate with his wife. Whitt went on to tell that he advised his wife to be careful of Buster.

When asked why he never mentioned his suspicions about his wife and Buster, Whitt answered it was "*simply because of the love I had for my wife and children. I thought I would rather be hung than let the jury know the truth*". Whitt insisted that he did not want to kill Buster, but feared for his life.

The Sunday before Christmas day, Whitt recited a different exchange between himself and Buster. As mentioned in the 1904 trial, Buster made remarks about Ms. Kizer and other women on the road including Whitt's wife. However, Whitt added that on that particular night, he left the room and upon returning he saw that Buster had kissed his wife. Whitt never said anything because Buster left. The next time he saw Buster was the morning of Christmas Eve at Mr. Scroggins' home. Whitt said that when Buster arrived at Scroggins' house that fateful morning, Buster told him that he had seen his wife that morning and "*she looked better than she ever did*".

Without Penalty   J.B. Jones

That specific remark was what made Whitt mad and he confronted Buster.

After describing the fight that occurred Christmas Eve morning, Whitt discussed shooting Buster. At this trial, Whitt gave a different account of meeting Buster in the road. He said that Buster stopped and said, *"Whitt, we had some trouble this morning and now would be a good time to settle it. One or the other of us must die"*. After this apparent threat, Buster allegedly put his hand in his pocket as if to grab his pistol. According to his testimony, it seemed that Buster could not get the pistol out on account of his overcoat. As a result, Whitt shot Buster before he could shoot him. Jim Whitt insisted that Buster was facing him when he fired the second shot and thought he was coming towards him.

Whitt ended his testimony by describing how he told his family that he had shot Buster and was going to turn himself in because it was justifiable. Jim Whitt truly believed that Buster Thomason was going to kill him.

Without Penalty   J.B. Jones

The state called several rebuttal witnesses to discredit Wat Luckett. Nevertheless, Watt Luckett's testimony apparently did not influence the jury. According to the May 12, 1905 edition of the Senatobia Democrat, *Friday morning about 11:00, the jury announced they had reached a verdict. When the 12 men filed into the courthouse a stillness followed that is characteristic of a solemn occasion. His Honor asked the foreman, if the jury had reached a verdict. The foreman announced in the affirmative and read: "We the jury, find the defendant guilty as charged in the indictment and fix his sentence at imprisonment for life in the state penitentiary." The jury was then discharged and the second trial of State of Mississippi against Jim Whitt closed.*

Because of this notorious case, the audience in the courtroom was large each day. The attorneys on both sides presented their prospective cases in a thorough and impressive way. However, the defense was not satisfied and promptly filed a appeal to the Mississippi Supreme Court again. The Senatobia Democrat reported this extraordinary decision to appeal the case - "*this will be the second time*

Without Penalty J.B. Jones

that the Whitt case will appear before the high court of the State, and if it is reversed Whitt will be tried the third time for killing Buster Thomason, on the 24th of December, 1903."

On February 6, 1906, the Supreme Court listened to arguments concerning the case of James "Jim" Whitt vs. the State of Mississippi.

According to the eBook - Cases Argued and Decided in the Mississippi Supreme Court Volume 87, W.J. East presented the following argument for the appellant: *"The remarks of the district attorney were in direct violation of law. It was the duty of the jury to try appellant on the evidence. The statement that he had been convicted before, and that the sentence was reversed on the merest technicality... was a calculated way to sway the jury. The reversal was not a matter with which they had anything to do, and such language should not have been used."* The assistant attorney-general only offered in rebuttal that *"the remarks of the district attorney...ought not to cause a reversal of the judgment now appealed from."*

Judge Calhoun delivered the opinion of the court:

Without Penalty   J.B. Jones

The district attorney, in his closing argument to the jury, said: "Every lawyer who deserves the name lawyer knows that the case was reversed by the Supreme Court on the merest technicality." Defendant objected at once to these remarks. Thereupon the district attorney turned to defendant's attorney and said loudly: "Yes, I said it. Write it out and sign my name to it. This case, gentlemen of the jury, was reversed on account of the absence of Wat Luckett, when the record shows by affidavits on file with the record that Wat Luckett was here at the trial." This, also, was objected to, but the court remained silent, did not sustain the objection, and exception was taken.

...The trial ceased to be fair when these words, seasonably objected to, were used without correction. Juries have no concern with the action of this court. The previous reversal of this case so far from being technical, was the very crux of an impartial trial..."

The April 6, 1906 edition of the Star Ledger - Kosciusko, Mississippi reported and explained the Supreme Court's decision, "*Because of an unfortunate remark made by the district attorney in his appeal to the jury, the Supreme Court has again*

Without Penalty J.B. Jones

reversed the famous Jim Whitt murder case, appellant having been twice convicted and sentenced to death for the murder of Buster Thomason...This case has attained unusual celebrity on account of the fact that it was in an attempt to save Whitt from the hands of an infuriated mob that Sheriff J.M. Poag lost his life, being shot down by members of the mob. Justice Calhoun read the decision of the court reversing the sentence for the second time, and chiefly because of the fact that the district attorney, addressing the jury, declared that the former reversal by the Supreme Court was purely on a technicality and did not involve the facts of the case; that the witness who was alleged to have been absent and whose testimony was declared to be essential to the defendant's case, was in the courtroom throughout the trial. Justice Calhoun said that when remarks of this character were unfair and impartial; that juries have nothing to do with the decisions of the Supreme Court are the grounds on which such decisions are rendered.

James "Jim" Whitt was granted yet another new trial in 1906.

Without Penalty   J.B. Jones

****

Because Jim Whitt appealed to the Mississippi Supreme Court, I was able to obtain copies of the transcripts from both the 1904 and 1905 trials from the Mississippi Archives. Having the actual transcripts provided an insight to this complex case that I could not get from a simple newspaper article. Obviously, the allegations on both sides are open for interpretation. I have tried not to form an opinion on the guilt or innocence of James Whitt. However, I do have a difficult time believing his assertion about his wife and Buster Thomason for the following reasons:

If you recall in the 1904 trial, J.J. Morris, Whitt's father-in-law briefly mentioned that Louisa had found out that Whitt had a living wife in Alabama. It is not hard to believe that Louisa might have heard about Whitt's first wife, Bell Hunter Whitt because the couple had moved to Alabama for a short time in 1902. When I began to research the possibility of

Without Penalty J.B. Jones

Whitt having another wife, I found that James Whitt had indeed married Bell Hunter in Lincoln County, Tennessee on March 5, 1888. I am not sure when exactly James Whitt moved to Mississippi. However, I know that he left Bell and three small children in 1895. In the 1900 census, Bell is listed as a widow living in Alabama with her brother's family and three children - Jessie, Charlie, and Eddie.

James Whitt married Louisa Morris in 1898 when she was 16 years old. He was most likely 30 years old at that time. The couple had 3 children together before he was arrested.

I have to speculate that Louisa found out about Whitt's first wife sometime after moving to Alabama. I have a copy of a summons filed in Alabama dated November 1902 - Bell Whitt vs James Whitt. In addition, I have the divorce decree dated February 3, 1903.

Upon seeking a divorce, Bell Whitt filed a deposition with the Chancery Clerk in Madison County, Alabama. In these documents, Bell asserted that James Whitt abandoned her and their 3 small children. I wonder if Louisa found the summons and heard rumors while in Alabama - away from her family and friends. If so, it leaves little doubt as to why she wanted to return home. Whitt testified in his trial that his wife wanted to come home and the couple had only been back in Mississippi a couple of weeks before the shooting.

7

The Final Trial of James Whitt

October 1906
State of Mississippi vs. James Whitt
Case #1862

    Judge - J.B. Boothe
    Prosecution - W.A. Roane

On October 26, 1906, testimony began in the final trial of James "Jim" Whitt. Unfortunately, I was unable to obtain the transcripts to this particular trial. However, the Senatobia Democrat - November 2, 1906 edition reported that *"the evidence in the case was the same as brought at the former trials."* Belle Brown, Henry Wilson, and Charlie Rochelle were all witnesses for the state again along with several members of the mob that killed Sheriff Poag -

Without Penalty   J.B. Jones

R.T. McConnell, Alex Nelson, and J.H. Thomason. I have to assume that something was very different at this trial because on October 31, 1906 - the jury announced a verdict of NOT GUILTY.

The November 2, 1906 edition of the Senatobia Democrat disclosed the decision by the jury in this article:
WHITT
Acquitted - Twice Tried for Murder and Convicted

"The lawyers in the Whitt case concluded their arguments late Tuesday afternoon and the case was given to the jury for final disposition. The twelve men were out all of Tuesday night and Wednesday morning brought in a verdict of not guilty.

The history of the Whitt case is fresh in the minds of our readers, hence there is no reason to publish it here. He was tried twice before. The first trial resulted in conviction and he was sentenced to hang. The case was appealed to the Supreme Court and reversed. He was convicted in the second trial and sentenced to the penitentiary for life. The case was again appealed and reversed in acquittal.

> *Whitt left Senatobia Wednesday morning on the south-bound train.*
>
> *The result of the Whitt case closes a chapter in the criminal history of Tate County that, doubtless, has no parallel in the south. It is hoped that it will forever stay closed and that this county will never have to experience a similar case."*

****

In March 1907, Louisa Morris Whitt filed a petition to the Chancery Court of Tate County requesting a divorce from James "Jim" Whitt.

In the first paragraph of the document, Louisa stated *"that she and the defendant were pretendedly married."* Furthermore, Louisa charged that after Whitt had been incarcerated in jail, she was advised that he was married to Bell Whitt and he had not been legally divorced. Therefore, the assertion made was that the marriage between Louisa and Jim was illegal and void because he had been married to another person.

As alluded to in the previous trials, the petition indicated that sometime prior Whitt's incarceration...Louisa had heard rumors of his marriage to another person. When she had asked Whitt about his previous marriage, he completely denied the rumors. However, Whitt did admit that he had been married before, but assured Louisa that he was legally divorced. Unfortunately, Louisa was living in Alabama which was hundreds of miles away from her family and unable to consult anyone for advice about this revelation.

In addition, Louisa mentioned the fact that Bell Whitt had begun the process to divorce Jim Whitt in November 1902. Louisa stated that she was aware of a summons for Jim Whitt, but did not understand exactly what the document meant until after her husband was placed in jail. Upon consulting her attorney and examining the summons, Louisa learned the truth about Jim Whitt.

I obtained a copy of the summons for James Whitt that was sent to Madison County, Alabama on March 12, 1907. Regrettably, it took until the next term of the Chancery Court for Louisa Whitt to be granted a divorce on September 10, 1907. Thankfully, Louisa was able to find happiness again by marrying a man named John T. Butler. As far as I can tell,

Without Penalty   J.B. Jones

Louisa and her three children by Jim Whitt never heard from him again.

As far as Jim Whitt, well, he married Bell Whitt again before his divorce was final from Louisa on July 20, 1907. He lived the remainder of his life with Bell in Madison County, Alabama.

8

The Mob Trials

Unlike the trials of Jim Whitt, I was unable to acquire any of the court transcripts from the mob trials. However, I did find a very detailed article published in the September 15, 1905 edition of the Commercial Appeal. The information from that particular article allowed me to summarize the first mob trial below:

The first of the three mob trials began in Holly Springs, Mississippi on August 25, 1905. J.H. Thomason, Sam Howell, R.T. McConnell, and Tom Vincent were the defendants. The state was represented by District Attorney W.A. Roane, Special Prosecutor (appointed by Governor Vardaman) - J.F. Dean, and Attorneys Smith & Totten from Holly

Springs. The defense attorneys were J.W. Lauderdale, J.L. Farley, R.E.L. Morgan, and W.S. Belk.

This case was followed with great interest across the area. Several witnesses from Tate County were summoned to appear at this trial. Among them was Bessie Poag, the widow of Sheriff Poag.

Mrs. Bessie Poag's testimony was spent reliving the moments leading up to her husband's murder. She described waking up to a noise outside the jail and someone calling out, "oh, Johnny!" The noise prompted her husband to get out of bed to investigate, but not before securing his pistol. Although Mrs. Poag remained in the bedroom, she could hear the exchange between a man claiming to be Bob Pickle and her husband before hearing gun shots. Mrs. Poag concluded her emotional testimony by describing the wounds in the sheriff's side and arm and hearing him calling out to her brother, "I am murdered. I am shot twice."

The next witness was Dr. Potter, the physician that attended to Sheriff Poag. The doctor explained that he arrived about one hour after the shooting. Dr. Potter described the sheriff's wounds and felt that either could have been fatal. Despite the prognosis, Sheriff Poag was entirely conscious and made voluntary statements to Dr. Potter about the shooting. As a result, the sheriff was able to order bloodhounds and describe his own murder. Sheriff Poag told the doctor that he was awakened by a rattling on the window and secured his pistol before checking outside. The sheriff said he questioned the man outside the jail before opening the door. However, when Sheriff Poag opened the door he saw a crowd of masked men which prompted him to throw up his pistol and shoot - aiming above them. Unfortunately, the men shot back.

Interestingly enough, Dr. Potter was called back to the courthouse a few days after the sheriff's murder to attend to Sam Howell in which the doctor removed *"what looked like a pistol ball that was over 48 hours old"*.

Other testimony included Acting Sheriff J.T. Gabbert. He divulged the details of the confession made by J.H. Thomason after his arrest. Upon arriving at the jail, Thomason allegedly said, "*I suppose the boys have given the whole thing away.*" Gabbert explained that he asked Thomason for a statement, but did not make any promises or threats. Thomason told him, "*It made no difference to him that he would soon have that bullet in his heart as to have gotten these boys into trouble.*" According to his confession, Thomason admitted that the ruse was to bring a prisoner to jail and claim to be Bob Pickle. If it worked, Sam Howell was to grab Poag and the others were to go upstairs to get Jim Whitt. Thomason also told Gabbert that he was certain Norman Clayton, one of the Spencer brothers, and Howell did the shooting.

After hearing all of this testimony, the defense attorneys began the cross-examination by accusing Gabbert of making false promises to Thomason in order to obtain a confession. Obviously, Gabbert unequivocally denied making any such statement. Nevertheless, the attorneys took it one step further by calling the defendant Thomson to explain that he had been coerced. Several witnesses were then called that had been present during the time Gabbert had questioned Thomason and all denied that any promises or threats were made. After all the discussion without the jury present about Thomason and Gabbert's conversation, Gabbert was allowed to continue with stating his recollection of R.T. McConnell's confession. Gabbert explained that he told McConnell the same thing - that he could make no promises, but wanted a statement. According to Gabbert, McConnell asked him if anyone else had confessed. Upon learning that the others had talked, McConnell divulged what happened that night to Gabbert and others.

At this point, the defense was not pleased and immediately introduced McConnell in rebuttal. McConnell said, *"that Gabbert told him he wanted to hear what he knew and that others had made a confession or taken advantage of a confession. And, Gabbert promised he would use his influence with the governor for him."* Of course, Gabbert was reintroduced and empathically denied making any inducements or saying anything about the governor to McConnell. After all the groveling over Gabbert's testimony, the court ruled that it should go before the jury. However, there was considerable time wrangling over the points of law on both sides. As a result, only four witnesses were allowed to testify on the first day of the trial.

The second day of the trial included an interesting revelation from T.P. Hill, a close friend of J.H. Thomason. Mr. Hill claimed that the defendant Thomson was depressed and felt the entire situation was a sad affair. Apparently, Thomason told Mr. Hill that the group had expected to get in the jail without hurting anyone. It was also mentioned in his testimony that Sheriff Poag had believed in Mr. Thomason. At some point, the sheriff had personally asked Mr. Thomason about the rumors of a lynching, but was assured that no mob would attempt such a feat. The witness alleged that this misplaced confidence in Thomason led to Sheriff Poag's death.

Other witnesses were called to discuss the aftermath of the murder of Sheriff Poag. Deputy Sheriff W.G. Lowery explained how he began the investigation, organized the posse, and secured evidence. He described the bullet marks at the jail and items found at Sam Howell's mill. Other deputies told about finding masks at Broom's gin which led the posse to the Strayhorn area.

Before the state rested their case, two final witnesses were called. J.A. Wooten, the Tate County Chancery Clerk, and R.C. Smith, the Tate County Circuit clerk. Both men testified that J.H. Thomason had requested them to speak to Sheriff Poag. They were asked to encourage Poag to keep Jim Whitt in the Senatobia jail because according to Thomason, "*if Whitt was removed, it would look like fear of a mob and make a bad impression of Poag.*" The two officials admitted to relaying this message to Sheriff Poag.

Tom Vincent, one of the defendants, was released at the start of the third day. After this development, the defense began to call a number of character witnesses. Each one was provided to attest to the good character of the defendants.

After hearing multiple witnesses, the state, possibly to keep things moving, offered to admit that the characters of all the defendants were good, but the defense declined. Besides the character of the defendants, the defense attempted "*to show that*

Without Penalty   J.B. Jones

Sheriff Poag was of a nervous and excitable temperament especially in the discharge of his duty". Thankfully, this attack was immediately objected to by the prosecution.

R.T. McConnell took to the stand in his own defense. McConnell asserted he had told Thomason that he would only be involved if Poag was not hurt. He considered Poag a good friend and was related to Mrs. Poag. His story was that Jack Spencer had knocked on the door of the jail. When the knock seemed to fail, J.H. Thomason had called out for the group to leave. He assumed everyone had heard the order to leave, but heard two shots come from the jail door. McConnell said he heard other shots as he was going away. He claimed that Poag fired from the door, but did not know who fired the other shots. Although he considered Poag one of the best friends he had in the county, McConnell agreed to participate in the attack.

Sam Howell who was wounded in the assault repeated the assertion that Sheriff Poag was not to be hurt in the attack on the jail. He stated that the sheriff fired first. Another former defendant, Tom Vincent basically reiterated Howell's statement that the sheriff was not to be hurt and Poag fired the first shots.

The last witness for the defense was J.H. Thomason. He was allegedly the leader of the mob. Thomason claimed that he saw Poag get a pistol and as a result, gave word for the crowd to disperse. He was not armed and did not know who fired at Poag. Furthermore, Thomason completely denied asking the Chancery Clerk and Circuit Clerk to speak to Poag about keeping Whitt in the Senatobia jail. He also dismissed the idea that he was the leader of the mob. Thomason accused Jack Spencer of being the leader of the mob. Interestingly enough, Jack Spencer had been found dead in May 1905 from a gunshot wound presumably from Sheriff Poag. After a few rebuttal witnesses, both sides rested. The newspaper article concluded with this statement: *"The defendants were placed on the stand today, first, because they were already on by confessions, and second, to show abandonment at the jail of the conspiracy to lynch Jim Whitt, in order that they might avail themselves with the right of self-defense."*

Without Penalty   J.B. Jones

On Tuesday, September 12, the Jackson Daily News; Jackson, Mississippi reported the following:

"The jury in the Poag case, after deliberating thirty-six hours, today returned a verdict of NOT GUILTY...

The theory advanced by the defense was that the mob thinking its efforts to deceive the sheriff had failed, had turned and started to leave when the officer opened the door and fired. Some member of the mob thereupon returned the fire and mortally wounded Poag. All of the defendants swore that they did not know who fired the fatal shot.

No trial in recent years has excited such interest...as the one just ended in acquittal. The verdict is somewhat of a surprise, as predictions made while the jury was deliberating were that it would be either a conviction or a hung jury."

****

The second mob trial began in Oxford, Mississippi on Monday, March 12, 1906. Alex Nelson, Oscar Manning, Henry Hunter, and Will Sinquefield were the defendants in the

Without Penalty   J.B. Jones

case. The state was represented by W.A. Roane and J.F. Dean. The defense attorneys were J.H. Farley, Shands & Stone, and J.W. Lauderdale.

Unfortunately, there were no detailed reports printed in any newspaper that I could find. I even traveled to the Oxford courthouse hoping to find something, but only found the minutes of the trial. I do not know the particulars that were presented by the state or defense, but I have one article from the March 30, 1906 edition of the Senatobia Democrat which stated - "*Alex Nelson, Henry Hunter, Oscar Manning, and Will Sinquefield were tried in the Circuit Court of Lafayette County last week upon a change of venue of killing the late Sheriff J.M. Poag in an attempt to lynch Jim Whitt. The trial consumed almost the entire week and was submitted to the jury at 12:00 p.m. on Friday. At a late hour on Saturday night, the jury reported that it was unable to agree and was discharged by the court and a mistrial entered.*" In the article, there were various reports given by the attorneys in the case as to where the jury stood, but it made no difference to me. The sad reality was that

Without Penalty   J.B. Jones

the trial ended in a mistrial and the state decided not to retry the case.

****

The third and final mob trial began in Batesville, Mississippi on Tuesday, April 17, 1906. William Still, Norman Clayton, and Will Smith were the defendants. Like the second mob trial, I do not have much information. I went to Batesville and was told that all the early records were destroyed in a fire. Therefore, I tried my best to find any newspaper article I could. The Senatobia Democrat published two very short articles in April 1906. One simply stated the case had begun and a large number of Tate County people had attended.

The second article from the April 27, 1906 issue led with this headline -
Boothe Scorned the Poag Jury
"The jury in the case of the State vs Norman Clayton, Williams Still and Dave Smith charged with killing Sheriff J.M. Poag at Senatobia about one year ago, which has been on trial here since Tuesday, returned a verdict of not guilty at

Without Penalty — J.B. Jones

4:30 this afternoon after a deliberation of about five hours.

Judge J.B. Boothe remarked to the jury when the verdict was read about as follows: Gentlemen: You were sworn to try this case according to the law and evidence, and to vindicate the law of the land; for some reason unknown to the court, you have disregarded your oaths and trampled the law under your feet. You are discharged."

****

9

Without Penalty

There is honestly not an appropriate way to end this story. It began with a tragic event and ended without any justice or penalty. When I discovered the outcome of this story, I was simply sad. It seems impossible to me that no one was held accountable. However, I hope that after reading this heartbreaking story - you can find a renewed sense of appreciation for our law enforcement officers and military that place themselves in harm's way every day.

May we never forget
Sheriff John Macon Poag
End of Watch - April 12, 1905

Without Penalty   J.B. Jones

****

    I periodically google "Sheriff J.M. Poag" and always tend to find the same information. Recently, I found an interesting article from an eBook about a musician from our area named Sid Hemphill.

    If you follow the Mississippi Blues Trail, it will take you Sid Hemphill's marker at Gabbert Park in Senatobia. Mr. Hemphill was recorded in 1945 by Alan Lomax. As Lomax and Hemphill discussed his music, Hemphill told a story of a man named Sam Howell (one of the members of the mob) who asked him to write a song. I was completely shocked when I read the words and listened to the song below:

The Strayhorn Mob

    Them boys around Strayhorn, they didn't have no job,
        Went to Senatoby, they had a big mob,
        Laid him low.

Without Penalty   J.B. Jones

    They went round to the jailhouse,
"Jailer! We wants the key,"
    Said, "Boys, if you gets the key, you gwine to have to murder me,"
    "We'll lay you low."

    Some walked round the jailhouse, stopped in at the gate,
    Some of 'em made a shot with a thirty-eight,
    They laid him low.

    Well, you talk about some runnin' then, all of 'em run just lake quails,
    Oughta been there to see them run, seen Mister Will Sinquefield,
    They laid him low.

    Well, they're talkin' 'bout that mob, hasn't been nary one since,
    Talkin' 'bout Mister Hunter, when he jumped the courtyard fence,
    And laid him low.

    Mister Norman Clayton, he told the boys, "Boys, now, if y'all all wait,

Without Penalty J.B. Jones

We'll soon get back to Strayhorn if we can follow a trottin' gait,"
They laid him low.

Senatoby boys was ragin' mad, but they didn't play so bad,
Scared to fool with the Strayhorn boys, Mister Sam Howell was bad,
He'll lay you low.

These Strayhorn boys, tell you boys, tell you-all a certain fact,
The hounds got on their tracks, and they brought the boys back,
But they laid him low.

When they tried the Strayhorn boys, they did not try 'em here,
Tried the boys most everywhere, but they all sure come clear,
They laid him low.

When they tried the Strayhorn boys, did not try 'em alone,
Tried the boys most everywhere, but they sure come home,

Without Penalty J.B. Jones

They laid him low.

Mister Norman Clayton, told the boys again, "Boys, if y'all have a little wait,
We'll soon get back to Strayhorn if we can follow a trottin' gait,"
They laid him low.

When the boys got to runnin' there, they didn't run like quails,
Oughta been there to see 'em run, seen Mister Will Sinquefield,
Laid him low.

****

Bibliography

"The Sheriff of Tate County Killed by Mob". *Jackson Daily News*, 12 April 1905, page 1

"A Sheriff is Killed". *The Commercial Appeal*, 12 April 1905, page 1

"Sheriff Poag Assassinated". *The Senatobia Democrat*, 12 April 1905, page 1

"Sheriff Killed". *The Roswell Daily Record*, 12 April 1905, page 1

"Sheriff Gives Up His Life to Save Prisoner". *The Piqua Daily Call*, 12 April 1905, page 1

"Plucky Sheriff is Shot to Death by 8 Masked Men". *The Charlotte News*, 12 April 1905, page 1

"Mississippi Sheriff Killed in the Jail". *San Francisco Chronicle*, 13 April 1905, page 5

"Sheriff Dies at Post". *Roseburg Review*, 13 April 1905, page 1

"Masked Men Kill Sheriff". *The Washington Post*, 13 April 1905, page 11

"Mob Kills Sheriff at Jail". *The New York Times*, 13 April 1905, page 1

"Tribute to Sheriff Poag". The Senatobia Democrat, 14 April 1905

"To Erect Home." *The Senatobia Democrat*, 21 April 1905

The Senatobia Democrat. 24 April 1905

"In Memory of John M. Poag". *The Senatobia Democrat*, 25 April 1905

"The Sheriff of Tate County Killed by Mob". *Jackson Daily News*, 12 April 1905

Without Penalty J.B. Jones

Robert Springer. Nobody Knows Where the Blues Come From: Lyrics and History, 2006. University Press of Mississippi

Cases Argued and Decided in the Supreme Court of Mississippi, Volume 87, 1906. E.W. Stephens Publishing Company

"To My Fellow Countymen". *The Senatobia Democrat*, 21 August 1903

"Decisions of Supreme Court". *Vicksburg Evening Post*, 1 February 1905

"The Sheriff of Tate County Killed by Mob". *Jackson Daily News*, 12 April 1905, page 1

"A Sheriff is Killed". *The Commercial Appeal*, 12 April 1905, page 1

"Sheriff Poag Assassinated". *The Senatobia Democrat*, 12 April 1905, page 1

"Sheriff Killed". *The Roswell Daily Record*, 12 April 1905, page 1

Without Penalty   J.B. Jones

"Sheriff Gives Up His Life to Save Prisoner". *The Piqua Daily Call*, 12 April 1905, page 1

"Plucky Sheriff is Shot to Death by 8 Masked Men". *The Charlotte News*, 12 April 1905, page 1

"Mississippi Sheriff Killed in the Jail". *San Francisco Chronicle*, 13 April 1905, page 5

"Sheriff Dies at Post". *Roseburg Review*, 13 April 1905, page 1

"Masked Men Kill Sheriff". *The Washington Post*, 13 April 1905, page 11

"Mob Kills Sheriff at Jail". *The New York Times*, 13 April 1905, page 1

"Tribute to Sheriff Poag". *The Senatobia Democrat*, 14 April 1905

"The Sheriff of Tate County Killed by Mob". *Jackson Daily News*, 12 April 1905

Without Penalty   J.B. Jones

"Poag's Murderers Are Place in Jail". *Vicksburg Evening Post*, 14 April 1905, page 1

"Tate County Sheriff Murdered by a Mob". The Columbus Commercial, 16 April 1905, pages 1;3

"To Erect Home." *The Senatobia Democrat*, 21 April 1905

"Court in Session". *The Senatobia Democrat*. 24 April 1905

"In Memory of John M. Poag". *The Senatobia Democrat*, 25 April 1905

"Eleven Men Arraigned for Killing Sheriff Poag". *The Senatobia Democrat*, 3 May 1905

"A Life Sentence". *The Senatobia Democrat*, 12 May 1905

"Trial of J.H. Thomason". *The Senatobia Democrat*, 5 September 1905

Without Penalty J.B. Jones

"Trial of J.H. Thomason". *The Commercial Appeal*, 15 September 1905

"Are Not Guilty". *Jackson Daily News*, 12 September 1905, page 4

"Could Not Agree." *The Senatobia Democrat*, 30 March 1906

"Boothe Scored the Poag Jury". *The Senatobia Democrat*, 27 April 1906

"Whitt Escapes Another Time". *The Star Ledger*, 6 April 1906, page 1

"Whitt". The Senatobia Democrat, 2 November 1906, page 1

Belle Whitt vs James Whitt. State of Alabama, Madison County. Chancery Court, Deposition, 10 December 1902

Belle Whitt vs James Whitt. State of Alabama, Madison County. Chancery Court, Decree of Divorce, 2 February 1903

Without Penalty   J.B. Jones

James M. Whitt and Belle Whitt. State of Alabama, Madison County. Marriage License, Volume 32, page 434

The Petition of L.E. Whitt vs Jas. Whitt. State of Mississippi, Tate County. Chancery Court, 10 September 1907

Robert Springer. Nobody Knows Where the Blues Come From: Lyrics and History, 2006. University Press of Mississippi

Cases Argued and Decided in the Supreme Court of Mississippi, Volume 87, 1906. E.W. Stephens Publishing Company

Jim Whitt vs. State of Mississippi, SC0000011316, (Mississippi Supreme Court)

Jim Whitt vs. State of Mississippi, SC0000011791, (Mississippi Supreme Court)

Without Penalty — J.B. Jones

About The Author

J.B. Jones developed an interest in genealogy which led her to research and collect information about her family. Her research ignited her passion for writing by desiring to tell the untold stories of the past. Jones resides in North Mississippi with her husband and daughter.

Made in the USA
Columbia, SC
26 May 2018